Healthy Air Fryer Recipes

Easy and Tasty Low-Fat Recipes to Fry, Bake, Grill and Roast with Your Air Fryer

Linda Wang

© **Copyright 2021 by Linda Wang - All rights reserved.**

The content contained within this book may not be reproduced, duplicated or transmitted without direct written permission from the author or the publisher.
Under no circumstances will any blame or legal responsibility be held against the publisher, or author, for any damages, reparation, or monetary loss due to the information contained within this book. Either directly or indirectly.

Legal Notice:
This book is copyright protected. This book is only for personal use. You cannot amend, distribute, sell, use, quote or paraphrase any part, or the content within this book, without the consent of the author or publisher.

Disclaimer Notice:
Please note the information contained within this document is for educational and entertainment purposes only. All effort has been executed to present accurate, up to date, and reliable, complete information. No warranties of any kind are declared or implied. Readers acknowledge that the author is not engaging in the rendering of legal, financial, medical or professional advice. The content within this book has been derived from various sources. Please consult a licensed professional before attempting any techniques outlined in this book.
By reading this document, the reader agrees that under no circumstances is the author responsible for any losses, direct or indirect, which are incurred as a result of the use of information contained within this document, including, but not limited to, — errors, omissions, or inaccuracies.

TABLE OF CONTENTS

INTRODUCTION 1

Spaghetti Squash Fritters 5

Puffed Egg Tarts 7

Broccoli Cheese Quiche 9

Fried Mushroom 11

Cheese Toast 13

Tomatoes and Cabbage Stew 14

Courgettes Casserole 16

Jicama Fries 18

Air Fried Green Tomatoes 20

Healthy Garlic Stuffed Mushrooms 22

Delicious Potatoes with Mediterranean Dipping Sauce 24

Easy Veggie Rolls 26

Special Grilled Cheese 28

Crumbed Cod 29

Creamy Salmon 31

Dill Salmon 32

Snapper Fillets 34

Clams and Potatoes 35

Glazed Turkey Breast 36

Chicken with Mushrooms 38

Chicken and Beer	40
Teriyaki Chicken	42
Pork Chops and Yogurt Sauce	43
Nutmeg Beef Mix	45
Sausage Meatballs	46
Beef and Plums	48
Sautéed Meat with Potatoes	50
Cheese Zucchini Boats	53
BBQ Pulled Mushrooms	55
Indian Potatoes	57
Sesame Mustard Greens	59
Veggie Rice	61
Rice and Beans Stuffed Bell Peppers	63
Italian Olives	65
Creamy Squash Soup	67
Chickpea Air fryer Soup	69
Jalapeño Bacon Cheese Bread	72
Ranch Dipped Fillets	74
Zucchini Air Fried Gratin	76
Sweet Cream Cheese Wontons	78
Mini Lava Cakes	80
Coconut Bars	82
Cream Doughnuts	84

Avocado Walnut Bread 86

Pumpkin Bars 88

Cinnamon Doughnuts 90

Strawberry Tart 92

Rum Cheesecake 94

Apple Pie 96

Coco Mug Cake 99

NOTES 101

INTRODUCTION

An Air Fryer is a magic revolutionized kitchen appliance that helps you fry with less or even no oil at all. This kind of product applies Rapid Air technology, which offers a new way to fry with less oil. This new invention cooks food through the circulation of superheated air and generates 80% low-fat food. Although the food is fried with less oil, you don't need to worry as the food processed by the Air Fryer still has the same taste like the food fried using the deep-frying method.

This technology uses a superheated element, which radiates heat close to the food and an exhaust fan in its lid to circulate airflow. An Air Fryer ensures that the food processed is cooked completely. The exhaust fan located at the top of the cooking chamber helps the food get the same heating temperature in every part quickly, resulting in a cooked food of better and healthier quality. Besides, cooking with an Air Fryer is also suitable for those individuals which are too busy or do not have enough time. For example, an Air Fryer only needs half a spoonful of oil and takes 10 minutes to serve a medium bowl of crispy French fries.

In addition to serving healthier food, an Air Fryer also provides some other benefits to you. Since an Air Fryer helps you fry using less oil or without oil for some kind of food, it automatically reduces the fat and cholesterol content in food. Indeed, no one will refuse to enjoy fried food without worrying about the greasy and fat content. Having fried food with no guilt is one of the pleasures of life. Besides having low fat and cholesterol, you save some amount of money by consuming oil sparingly, which can be used for other needs. An Air Fryer also can reheat your food. Sometimes, when you have fried leftover and you reheat it, it will usually serve reheated greasy food with some addition of unhealthy reuse oil. Undoubtedly, the saturated fat in the fried food gets worse because of this process. An Air Fryer helps you reheat your food without being afraid of extra oils that the food may absorb. Fried bananas, fish and chips, nuggets, or even fried chicken can be reheated to become as warm and crispy as they were before by using an Air Fryer.

Some people may think that spending some amount of money to buy a fryer is wasteful. I dare to say that they are wrong because an Air Fryer is not only used to fry. It is a sophisticated multi-function appliance since it also helps you to roast chicken, make steak, grill fish, and even bake a cake. With a built-in air filter, an Air Fryer filters the air and saves your kitchen from smoke and grease.

An air Fryer is really a new innovative method of cooking. Grab it fast and welcome to a clean and healthy kitchen.

Spaghetti Squash Fritters

Preparation Time: 23 minutes

Servings: 4

Ingredients:

- 2 cups cooked spaghetti squash
- 1 large egg.
- 2 stalks green onion, sliced
- ¼ cup blanched finely ground almond flour.

- ½ tsp. garlic powder.
- 2 tbsp. unsalted butter; softened.
- 1 tsp. dried parsley.

Directions:

1. Remove excess moisture from the squash using a cheesecloth or kitchen towel.
2. Mix all ingredients in a large bowl. Form into four patties
3. Cut a piece of parchment to fit your air fryer basket. Place each patty on the parchment and place into the air fryer basket
4. Adjust the temperature to 400 Degrees F and set the timer for 8 minutes. Flip the patties halfway through the cooking time. Serve warm.

Nutrition:

Calories: 131; Protein: 3.8g; Fiber: 2.0g; Fat: 10.1g; Carbs: 7.1g

Puffed Egg Tarts

Preparation Time: 10 minutes

Cooking Time: 42 minutes

Servings: 4

Ingredients:

- 4 large eggs
- 1 sheet frozen puff pastry half, thawed and cut into 4 squares
- ¾ cup Monterey Jack cheese, shredded and divided
- 1 tablespoon fresh parsley, minced
- 1 tablespoon olive oil

Directions:

1. Preheat the Air fryer to 390 degrees F
2. Place 2 pastry squares in the air fryer basket and cook for about 10 minutes.
3. Remove Air fryer basket from the Air fryer and press each square gently with a metal tablespoon to form an indentation.

4. Place 3 tablespoons of cheese in each hole and top with 1 egg each.
5. Return Air fryer basket to Air fryer and cook for about 11 minutes.
6. Remove tarts from the Air fryer basket and sprinkle with half the parsley.
7. Repeat with remaining pastry squares, cheese and eggs.
8. Dish out and serve warm.

Nutrition:

Calories: 246, Fat: 19.4g, Carbohydrates: 5.9g, Sugar: 0.6g, Protein: 12.4g, Sodium: 213mg

Broccoli Cheese Quiche

Preparation Time: 10 minutes

Cooking Time: 40 minutes

Servings: 2

Ingredients:

- 1 large broccoli, chopped into florets
- 1 cup cheddar cheese, grated
- 3 large carrots, peeled and diced
- 2 large eggs
- ¼ cup feta cheese
- 1 teaspoon dried rosemary
- 1 teaspoon dried thyme
- Salt and black pepper, to taste

Directions:

1. Preheat the Air fryer to 360 degrees F and grease a quiche dish.
2. Place broccoli and carrots into a food steamer and cook for about 20 minutes until soft.
3. Whisk together eggs with milk, dried herbs, salt

and black pepper in a bowl.

4. Place steamed vegetables at the bottom of the quiche pan and top with tomatoes and cheese.
5. Drizzle with the egg mixture and transfer the quiche dish in the Air fryer.
6. Cook for about 20 minutes and dish out to serve warm.

Nutrition:

Calories: 412, Fat: 28, Carbohydrates: 16.3g, Sugar: 7.5g, Protein: 25.3g, Sodium: 720mg

Fried Mushroom

Preparation Time: 25 minutes

Servings: 4

- **Ingredients:**
- 4 eggs
- 7 oz. spinach; torn
- 4 slices bacon; chopped.
- 8 cherry tomatoes; halved
- 8 white mushrooms; sliced

- 1 garlic clove; minced
- A drizzle of olive oil
- Salt and black pepper to taste

Directions:

1. In a pan greased with oil and that fits your air fryer, mix all ingredients except for the spinach; stir.
2. Put the pan in your air fryer and cook at 400 °F for 15 minutes. Add the spinach, toss and cook for 5 minutes more. Divide between plates and serve

Cheese Toast

Preparation Time: 13 minutes

Servings: 2

Ingredients:

- 4 bread slices
- 4 cheddar cheese slices
- 4 tsp. butter; softened

Directions:

1. Spread the butter on each slice of bread. Place 2 cheese slices each on 2 bread slices, then top with the other 2 bread slices; cut each in half
2. Arrange the sandwiches in your air fryer's basket and cook at 370°F for 8 minutes. Serve hot and enjoy!

Tomatoes and Cabbage Stew

Preparation Time: 25 minutes

Servings: 4

Ingredients:

- 1 green cabbage head; shredded
- 14 oz. canned tomatoes; chopped.

- 4 oz. chicken stock
- 1 tbsp. sweet paprika
- 2 tbsp. dill; chopped.
- Salt and black pepper to taste.

Directions:

1. In a pan that fits your air fryer, mix the cabbage with the tomatoes and all the other ingredients except the dill, toss, introduce the pan in the fryer and cook at 380 °F for 20 minutes
2. Divide into bowls and serve with dill sprinkled on top.

Nutrition:

Calories: 200; Fat: 8g; Fiber: 3g; Carbs: 4g; Protein: 6g

Courgettes Casserole

Preparation Time: 25 minutes

Servings: 4

Ingredients:

- 2 courgettes; sliced
- 2 spring onions; chopped.
- 3 garlic cloves; minced
- 14 oz. cherry tomatoes; cubed

- 2 celery sticks; sliced
- ½ cup mozzarella; shredded
- 1 yellow bell pepper; chopped.
- 1 tbsp. thyme; dried
- 1 tbsp. olive oil
- 1 tsp. smoked paprika

Directions:

1. In a baking dish that fits your air fryer, mix all the ingredients except the cheese and toss.
2. Sprinkle the cheese on top, introduce the dish in your air fryer and cook at 380 °F for 20 minutes. Divide between plates and serve for lunch

Nutrition:

Calories: 254; Fat: 12g; Fiber: 2g; Carbs: 4g; Protein: 11g

Jicama Fries

Preparation Time: 30 minutes

Servings: 4

Ingredients:

- 1 small jicama; peeled.
- ¾tsp. chili powder
- ¼ tsp. onion powder.
- ¼ tsp. ground black pepper
- ¼ tsp. garlic powder.

Directions:

1. Cut jicama into matchstick-sized pieces.
2. Place pieces into a small bowl and sprinkle with remaining ingredients. Place the fries into the air fryer basket
3. Adjust the temperature to 350 Degrees F and set the timer for 20 minutes. Toss the basket two or three times during cooking. Serve warm.

Nutrition:

Calories: 37; Protein: 0.8g; Fiber: 4.7g; Fat: 0.1g; Carbs: 8.7g

Air Fried Green Tomatoes

Preparation Time: 17 minutes

Servings: 4

Ingredients:

- 1 large egg.
- 2 medium green tomatoes
- ⅓ cup grated Parmesan cheese.
- ¼ cup blanched finely ground almond flour.

Directions:

1. Slice tomatoes into ½-inch-thick slices. Take a medium bowl, whisk the egg. Take a large bowl, mix the almond flour and Parmesan.
2. Dip each tomato slice into the egg, then dredge in the almond flour mixture. Place the slices into the air fryer basket
3. Adjust the temperature to 400 Degrees F and set the timer for 7 minutes. Flip the slices halfway through the cooking time. Serve immediately

Nutrition:

Calories: 106; Protein: 6.2g; Fiber: 1.4g; Fat: 6.7g; Carbs: 5.9g

Healthy Garlic Stuffed Mushrooms

Preparation Time: 25 minutes

Servings: 2

Ingredients:

- 6 mushrooms [small]
- 1 tablespoon breadcrumbs
- 1 ounce. onion [peeled; diced]
- 1 tablespoon oil [olive]

- 1 teaspoon parsley
- 1 teaspoon garlic [pureed]
- salt to taste
- pepper to taste

Directions:

1. Mix breadcrumbs, oil, onion, parsley, salt, pepper and garlic in a medium sized bowl. Remove middle stalks from mushrooms and fill them with crumb mixture.
2. Cook in Air Fryer for 10 minutes at 350 - degrees Fahrenheit. Serve with mayo dip and enjoy the right combination.

Delicious Potatoes with Mediterranean Dipping Sauce

Preparation Time: 55 minutes

Servings: 4

Ingredients:

- 1 ½ tablespoons melted butter
- 2 pounds Russet potatoes; peeled and cubed
- 1 teaspoon sea salt flakes
- 2 sprigs thyme; leaves only, crushed
- 1 sprig rosemary; leaves only, crushed
- 1/2 teaspoon freshly cracked black peppercorns

For Mediterranean Dipping Sauce:

- 1/2 cup mascarpone cheese
- 1/3 cup yogurt
- 1 tablespoon fresh dill; chopped
- 1 tablespoon olive oil

Directions:

1. First; set your Air Fryer to cook at 350 - degrees Fahrenheit.
2. Now; add the potato cubes to the bowl with cold water and soak them approximately for 35 minutes.
3. After that; dry the potato cubes using a paper towel.
4. In a mixing dish; thoroughly whisk the melted butter with sea salt flakes, rosemary, thyme, and freshly cracked peppercorns.
5. Rub the potato cubes with this butter/spice mix.
6. Air-fry the potato cubes in the cooking basket for 18 to 20 minutes or until cooked through, make sure to shake the potatoes to cook them evenly.
7. Meanwhile; make the Mediterranean dipping sauce by mixing the remaining ingredients.
8. Serve warm potatoes with Mediterranean sauce for dipping and enjoy

Easy Veggie Rolls

Preparation Time: 30 minutes

Servings: 1

Ingredients:

- 1/4 cup peas
- 2 potatoes [mashed]
- 1/4 cup carrots [mashed]
- 1/4 beans
- 1 cabbage [small; sliced]
- 2 tablespoon sweet corn
- 1 onion [small; chopped]
- 1 teaspoon coriander
- 1 teaspoon capsicum
- 2 tablespoon butter
- ginger garlic to taste
- 1/2 teaspoon masala powder
- 1/2 teaspoon chili powder
- 1/2 cup breadcrumbs

- 1 packet roll sheets
- 1/2 cup cornstarch slurry

Directions:

1. Boil all the vegetables in half cup of water on a low heat and let them dry.
2. Spread the roll sheet and place the filling onto it then make the fillings into rolls and coat the rolls with slurry and breadcrumbs.
3. Preheat Air Fryer to 390 - degrees Fahrenheit and cook it for 10 minutes. Serve with boiled rice and have a treat.

Special Grilled Cheese

Preparation Time: 25 minutes

Servings: 2

Ingredients:

- 1/2 cup sharp cheddar cheese
- 4 slices of brioche or white bread
- 1/4 cup butter; melted

Directions:

1. Preheat the Air Fryer to 360 - degrees Fahrenheit. Place cheese and butter in separate bowls. Brush the butter on each side of the 4 slices of bread.
2. Place the cheese on 2 of the 4 pieces of bread. Put the grilled cheese together and add to the cooking basket.
3. Cook for 5 – 7 minutes or until golden brown and the cheese has melted.

Crumbed Cod

Preparation Time: 15 minutes

Cooking Time: 7 minutes

Servings: 4

Ingredients:

- 4: 4-ounceskinless codfish fillets, cut into rectangular pieces
- 6 eggs
- 1 cup flour

- 2 green chilies, finely chopped
- 6 scallions, finely chopped
- 4 garlic cloves, minced
- Salt and black pepper, to taste
- 2 teaspoons soy sauce

Directions:

1. Preheat the Air fryer to 375 degree F and grease an Air fryer basket.
2. Place the flour in a shallow dish and mix the remaining ingredients except cod in another shallow dish.
3. Coat each cod fillet into the flour and then dip in the egg mixture.
4. Arrange the cod fillets in the Air fryer basket and cook for about 7 minutes.
5. Dish out and serve warm.

Nutrition:

Calories: 462, Fat: 16.9g, Carbohydrates: 51.3g, Sugar: 3.3g, Protein: 24.4g, Sodium: 646mg

Creamy Salmon

Preparation time: 15 minutes

Servings: 2

Ingredients:

- Salmon: .75 lb. - 6 pieces
- Olive oil: 1 tbsp.
- Sour cream: 3 tbsp.
- Chopped dill: 1 tbsp.
- Plain yogurt: 1.75 oz.
- Salt: 1 pinch

Directions:

1. Program the temperature setting on the Air Fryer to 285º Fahrenheit.
2. Pour oil into the fryer basket. Shake the salt over the salmon and add it to the fryer basket. Air fry for 10 minutes.
3. Whisk the yogurt, dill, and salt.
4. Serve the salmon with the sauce and your favorite sides.

Dill Salmon

Preparation time: 30 minutes

Servings: 4

Ingredients:

- Salmon: 4 - 6-oz. pieces or 1.5 lb.
- Salt: 1 pinch
- Olive oil: 2 tsp.

Ingredients - The Sauce:

- Sour cream: .5 cup
- Non-fat Greek yogurt: .5 cup
- Dill: 2 finely chopped tbsp.
- Salt: 1 pinch

Directions:

1. Preheat the Air Fryer prior to baking time: 270º Fahrenheit).
2. Chop the salmon into the four portions. Drizzle with about half of the oil: 1 tsp.). Flavor with a pinch of salt and add to the basket for about 20-23 minutes.
3. Lastly, blend the yogurt, salt, sour cream, and dill in a mixing container. Pour the sauce over the cooked salmon with a pinch of chopped dill.

Snapper Fillets

Preparation Time: 20 minutes

Servings: 4

Ingredients:

- 8 garlic cloves; minced
- 4 medium snapper fillets; boneless
- 1/3 cup olive oil
- Juice of 2 limes
- 1 tbsp. lemon zest
- 1½ tbsp. green olives; pitted and sliced
- Salt and black pepper to taste

Directions:

1. Add all the ingredients except the fish to a baking dish that fits your air fryer; mix well.
2. Add the fish and toss gently, then place in the fryer
3. Cook at 360°F for 15 minutes. Divide everything between plates and serve

Clams and Potatoes

Preparation Time: 20 minutes

Servings: 4

Ingredients:
- 1 lb. baby red potatoes; scrubbed
- 15 small clams; shucked
- 2 tbsp. cilantro; chopped.
- 2 chorizo links; sliced
- 10 oz. beer
- 1 yellow onion; chopped.
- 1 tsp. olive oil

Directions:
1. In a pan that fits your air fryer, add all of the ingredients and toss
2. Place the pan in the fryer and cook at 390°F for 15 minutes. Divide into bowls and serve.

Glazed Turkey Breast

Preparation Time: 15 minutes

Cooking Time: 55 minutes

Servings: 8

Ingredients:

- 1: 5-poundsboneless turkey breast
- 1 teaspoon dried thyme, crushed
- 1 tablespoon butter, softened
- ½ teaspoon dried sage, crushed
- ½ teaspoon smoked paprika
- 2 teaspoons olive oil
- ¼ cup maple syrup
- 2 tablespoons Dijon mustard
- Salt and ground black pepper, as required

Directions:

1. Preheat the Air fryer to 350 degree F and grease an Air fryer basket.

2. Mix the herbs, paprika, salt, and black pepper in a bowl.
3. Drizzle the turkey breast with oil and season with the herb mixture.
4. Arrange the turkey breast into the Air Fryer basket and cook for about 50 minutes, flipping twice in between.
5. Meanwhile, mix the maple syrup, mustard, and butter in a bowl.
6. Coat the turkey evenly with maple glaze and cook for about 5 minutes.
7. Dish out the turkey breast onto a cutting board and cut into desired size slices to serve.

Nutrition:

Calories: 302, Fat: 3.3g, Carbohydrates: 5.6g, Sugar: 4.7g, Protein: 56.2g, Sodium: 170mg

Chicken with Mushrooms

Preparation Time: 10 minutes

Cooking Time: 24 minutes

Serve: 4

Ingredients:

- 1/3 cup sun-dried tomatoes
- 2 lbs chicken breasts, halved
- 8 oz mushrooms, sliced

- 1/2 cup mayonnaise
- 1 tsp salt

Directions:

1. Preheat the air fryer to 370 °F.
2. Spray air fryer baking dish with cooking spray.
3. Place chicken breasts into the baking dish and top with sun-dried tomatoes, mushrooms, mayonnaise, and salt. Mix well.
4. Place dish in the air fryer and cook for 24 minutes.
5. Serve and enjoy.

Nutrition:

Calories 561, Fat 26.8 g, Carbohydrates 9 g, Sugar 3.2 g, Protein 65 g, Cholesterol 209 mg

Chicken and Beer

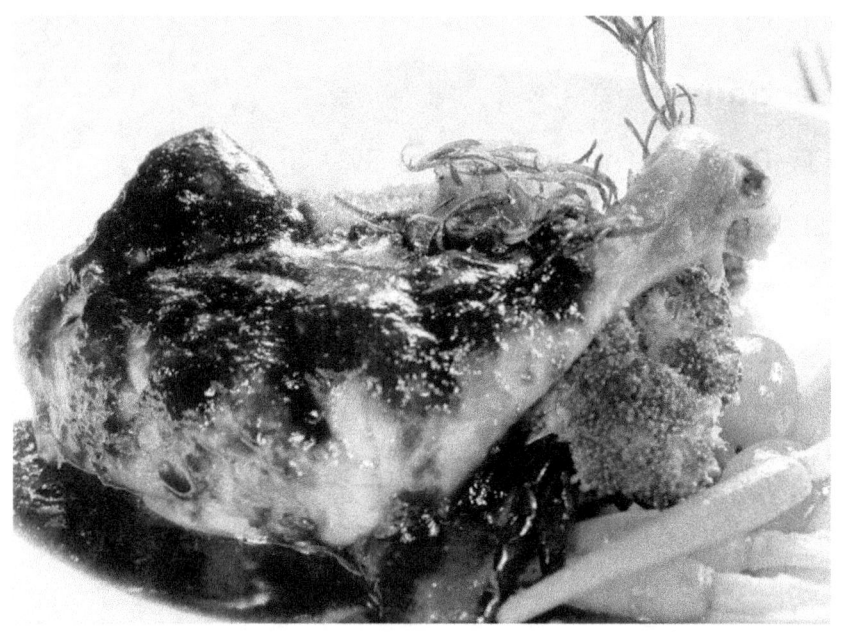

Preparation Time: 40 minutes

Servings: 4

Ingredients:

- 4 chicken drumsticks
- 1 yellow onion; minced
- 15 oz. beer
- 1 chili pepper; chopped.

- 2 tbsp. olive oil
- 1 tbsp. balsamic vinegar
- Salt and black pepper to taste

Directions:

1. Put the oil in a pan that fits your air fryer and heat up over medium heat.
2. Add the onion and the chili pepper, stir and cook for 2 minutes
3. Add the vinegar, beer, salt and pepper; stir and cook for 3 more minutes
4. Add the chicken, toss and put the pan in the fryer and cook at 370 °F for 20 minutes. Divide everything between plates and serve.

Teriyaki Chicken

Cooking Time: 14 minutes

Servings: 2

Ingredients:

- 2 boneless; skinless chicken thighs
- 3 tbsp. teriyaki sauce
- 1 tsp. ginger; grated.
- 1 tbsp. cooking wine

Directions:

1. Mix all ingredients in a bowl. Place bowl in the fridge for 30 minutes. Add marinated chicken to air fryer in a baking pan and cook at 350 °F for 8 minutes
2. After 8 minutes, flip the chicken over and cook for an additional 6 minutes. Serve hot.

Pork Chops and Yogurt Sauce

Preparation time: 10 minutes

Cooking time: 30 minutes

Servings: 4

Ingredients:

- 2pounds pork chops
- 2tablespoons avocado oil
- 1 cup yogurt

- 2garlic cloves, minced
- 1teaspoon turmeric powder
- 2tablespoon oregano, chopped
- Salt and black pepper to the taste

Directions:

1. In the air fryer's pan, mix the pork chops with the yogurt and the other ingredients, toss and cook at 400 degrees F for 30 minutes.
2. Divide the mix between plates and serve.

Nutrition:

Calories 301, Fat 7, Fiber 5, Carbs 19, Protein 22

Nutmeg Beef Mix

Preparation time: 10 minutes

Cooking time: 30 minutes

Servings: 4

Ingredients:

- 2pounds beef stew meat, cubed
- 2tablespoons avocado oil
- 1teaspoon nutmeg, ground
- ½ teaspoon chili powder
- ¼ cup beef stock
- Salt and black pepper to the taste
- 2tablespoons chives, chopped

Directions:

1. In a pan that fits your air fryer, mix the beef with the nutmeg and the other ingredients, toss, introduce the pan in the fryer and cook at 400 degrees F for 30 minutes.
2. Divide the mix into bowls and serve.

Nutrition:

Calories 280, Fat 12, Fiber 2, Carbs 17, Protein 14

Sausage Meatballs

Preparation Time: 15 minutes

Cooking Time: 15 minutes

Servings: 4

Ingredients:

- 3½-ounce sausage, casing removed
- 1 teaspoon fresh sage, chopped finely
- ½ medium onion, minced finely
- 3 tablespoons Italian breadcrumbs
- ½ teaspoon garlic, minced
- Salt and black pepper, to taste

Directions:

1. Preheat the Air fryer to 355 degrees F and grease an Air fryer basket.
2. Mix all the ingredients in a bowl until well combined.
3. Shape the mixture into equal-sized balls and arrange the balls in the Air fryer basket.
4. Cook for about 15 minutes and dish out to serve warm.

Nutrition:

Calories: 111, Fat: 7.3g, Carbohydrates: 5.2g, Sugar: 0.9g, Protein: 5.7g, Sodium: 224mg

Beef and Plums

Preparation Time: 50 minutes

Servings: 6

Ingredients:

- 8 oz. beef stock
- 1½ lbs. beef stew meat; cubed
- 9 oz. plums; pitted and halved

- 1 tsp. ginger powder
- 1 tsp. turmeric powder
- 1 tsp. cinnamon powder
- 2 yellow onions; chopped.
- 2 garlic cloves; minced
- 3 tbsp. honey
- 2 tbsp. olive oil
- Salt and black pepper to tastes

Directions:

1. In a pan that fits your air fryer, heat up the oil over medium heat.
2. Add the beef, stir and brown for 2 minutes
3. Add the honey, onions, garlic, salt, pepper, turmeric, ginger and cinnamon; toss and cook for 2-3 minutes more
4. Add the plums and the stock; toss again.
5. Place the pan in the fryer and cook at 380°F for 30 minutes. Divide everything into bowls and serve

Sautéed Meat with Potatoes

Preparation time: 20 minutes,

Cooking time: 45 minutes;

Serve: 6

Ingredients

- 750g beef
- 350 g of potatoes
- 250 g of tomato coulis
- 200 ml of hot broth
- 1 onion
- Salt to taste
- Pepper to taste

Directions:

1. Chop the onion and put it in the basket previously greased.
2. Set the temperature to 150 °C.
3. Brown the onion for 3 to 4 minutes and then add the pieces of meat, broth, salt, and pepper.

4. Cook the meat for 20 minutes and add the potatoes and the tomato coulis.
5. Cook for another 20 to 25 minutes, mixing the sautéed with a wooden spoon 3 to 4 times during cooking to prevent it from drying out too much.

Nutrition:

Calories 317, Carbohydrates 13g, Fat 18g, Sugars 1g, Protein 24g, Cholesterol 73mg

Cheese Zucchini Boats

Preparation Time: 35 minutes

Servings: 2

Ingredients:

- 2 medium zucchini
- ¼ cup full-fat ricotta cheese
- ¼ cup low-carb, no-sugar-added pasta sauce.
- ¼ cup shredded mozzarella cheese
- 2 tbsp. grated vegetarian Parmesan cheese
- ¼ tsp. garlic powder.
- 1 tbsp. avocado oil
- ½ tsp. dried parsley.
- ¼ tsp. dried oregano.

Directions:

1. Cut off 1-inch from the top and bottom of each zucchini.
2. Slice zucchini in half lengthwise and use a spoon to scoop out a bit of the inside, making room for filling. Brush with oil and spoon 2 tbsp. pasta

sauce into each shell

3. Take a medium bowl, mix ricotta, mozzarella, oregano, garlic powder and parsley
4. Spoon the mixture into each zucchini shell. Place stuffed zucchini shells into the air fryer basket.
5. Adjust the temperature to 350 Degrees F and set the timer for 20 minutes
6. To remove from the fryer basket, use tongs or a spatula and carefully lift out. Top with Parmesan. Serve immediately.

Nutrition:

Calories: 215; Protein: 10.5g; Fiber: 2.7g; Fat: 14.9g; Carbs: 9.3g

BBQ Pulled Mushrooms

Preparation Time: 17 minutes

Servings: 2

Ingredients:

- 4 large portobello mushrooms
- 1 tbsp. salted butter; melted.
- ½ cup low-carb, sugar-free barbecue sauce
- 1 tsp. paprika
- ¼ tsp. onion powder.
- ¼ tsp. ground black pepper
- 1 tsp. chili powder
-

Directions:

1. Remove stem and scoop out the underside of each mushroom. Brush the caps with butter and sprinkle with pepper, chili powder, paprika and onion powder.
2. Place mushrooms into the air fryer basket. Adjust the temperature to 400 Degrees F and set the timer for 8 minutes.

3. When the timer beeps, remove mushrooms from the basket and place on a cutting board or work surface. Using two forks, gently pull the mushrooms apart, creating strands.
4. Place mushroom strands into a 4-cup round baking dish with barbecue sauce. Place dish into the air fryer basket.
5. Adjust the temperature to 350 Degrees F and set the timer for 4 minutes. Stir halfway through the cooking time. Serve warm.

Nutrition:

Calories: 108; Protein: 3.3g; Fiber: 2.7g; Fat: 5.9g; Carbs: 10.9g

Indian Potatoes

Preparation Time: 10 minutes

Cooking duration: 12 minutes

Servings: 4

Ingredients:

- 1 tablespoon coriander seeds
- 1 tablespoon cumin seeds
- ½ teaspoon red chili powder
- ½ teaspoon turmeric powder
- 1 teaspoon pomegranate powder
- 1 tablespoon pickled mango, chopped
- 2 teaspoons fenugreek, dried
- 5 potatoes, boiled, peeled and cubed
- 2 tablespoons olive oil
- Salt and black pepper to the taste

Directions:

1. Heat up a pan that fits your air fryer with the oil over medium heat, add coriander and cumin seeds, stir and cook for 2 minutes.
2. Add salt, pepper, turmeric, chili powder, pomegranate powder, mango, fenugreek and potatoes, toss, introduce in your air fryer and cook at 360 °F for 10 minutes.
3. Divide among plates and serve hot.

Nutrition:

Calories: 100; Fat: 7g; Fiber: 3g; Carbs: 4g; Protein: 5g

Sesame Mustard Greens

Preparation Time: 10 minutes

Cooking duration: 11 minutes

Servings: 4

Ingredients:

- 1 pound mustard greens, torn
- 2 garlic cloves, minced
- 1 tablespoon olive oil

- ½ cup yellow onion, sliced
- 3 tablespoons veggie stock
- ¼ teaspoon dark sesame oil
- Salt and black pepper to the taste

Directions:

1. Heat up a pan that fits your air fryer with the oil over medium heat, add onions, stir and brown them for 5 minutes.
2. Add garlic, stock, greens, salt and pepper, stir, introduce in your air fryer and cook at 350 °F for 6 minutes.
3. Add sesame oil, toss to coat, divide among plates and serve.

Nutrition:

Calories: 173; Fat: 6g; Fiber: 2g; Carbs: 4g; Protein: 5g

Veggie Rice

Preparation Time: 20 minutes

Cooking Time: 18 minutes

Servings: 2

Ingredients:

- 2 cups cooked white rice
- 1 large egg, lightly beaten
- ½ cup frozen carrots, thawed
- ½ cup frozen peas, thawed
- ½ teaspoon sesame seeds, toasted
- 1 tablespoon vegetable oil
- 1 tablespoon water
- 2 teaspoons sesame oil, toasted and divided
- Salt and ground white pepper, as required
- 1 teaspoon soy sauce
- 1 teaspoon Sriracha sauce

Directions:

1. Preheat the Air fryer to 380 degrees F and grease an Air fryer pan.
2. Mix the rice, vegetable oil, 1 teaspoon of sesame oil, water, salt, and white pepper in a bowl.
3. Transfer the rice mixture into the Air fryer basket and cook for about 12 minutes.
4. Pour the beaten egg over rice and cook for about 4 minutes.
5. Stir in the peas and carrots and cook for 2 more minutes.
6. Meanwhile, mix soy sauce, Sriracha sauce, sesame seeds and the remaining sesame oil in a bowl.
7. Dish out the potato cubes onto serving plates and drizzle with sauce to serve.

Nutrition:

Calories: 163, Fat: 8.4g, Carbohydrates: 15.5g, Sugar: 11.2g, Protein: 6.4g, Sodium: 324mg

Rice and Beans Stuffed Bell Peppers

Preparation Time: 30 minutes

Servings: 5

Ingredients:

- 1/2 cup mozzarella cheese, shredded
- 5 large bell peppers, tops removed and seeded
- 1/2 small bell pepper, seeded and chopped
- 1: 15-ozcan red kidney beans, rinsed and drained
- 1: 15-ozcan diced tomatoes with juice
- 1 tbsp. Parmesan cheese; grated
- 1 cup cooked rice
- 1 ½ tsp. Italian seasoning

Directions:

1. In a bowl; mix well chopped bell pepper, tomatoes with juice, beans, rice and Italian seasoning. Stuff each bell pepper evenly with the rice mixture.

2. Set the temperature of air fryer to 360 °F. Grease an air fryer basket.
3. Arrange bell peppers into the air fryer basket in a single layer.
4. Air fry for about 12 minutes. Meanwhile, in a bowl, mix together the mozzarella and Parmesan cheese.
5. Remove the air fryer basket and top each bell pepper with cheese mixture. Air fry for 3 more minutes.
6. Remove from air fryer and transfer the bell peppers onto a serving platter. Set aside to cool slightly. Serve warm.

Italian Olives

Preparation Time: 20 minutes

Servings: 4

Ingredients

- 2 cups black olives, pitted and halved
- 12 oz. tomatoes; chopped.
- 4 garlic cloves; minced
- 2 red bell peppers; sliced
- 2 rosemary springs; chopped.

- A handful basil; chopped.
- 2 tbsp. olive oil

Directions:

1. In a pan that fits the air fryer, combine the olives with the rest of the ingredients, toss.
2. Put the pan in the fryer and cook at 380 °F for 15 minutes
3. Divide between plates and serve.

Nutrition:

Calories: 173; Fat: 6g; Fiber: 2g; Carbs: 4g; Protein: 5g

Creamy Squash Soup

Preparation Time: 5 minutes

Cooking Time: 15 minutes

Servings: 4

Ingredients:

- 4 cups beef stock
- 4 lbs. butternut squash, peeled, seeded, and cubed
- 1 tsp. thyme
- ½ tsp. sage
- 2 garlic cloves, minced
- 1 onion, chopped
- 2 tbsp. olive oil
- Pepper
- Salt

Directions:

1. Add oil into air fryer and set on Sauté mode.
2. Add garlic and onion to the pot. Sauté for 5 minutes.
3. Add sage, thyme, pepper and salt. Stir for a minute.
4. Add squash and stock. Stir well.
5. Secure pot with lid and cook on manual high pressure for 10 minutes.
6. Quick release pressure then open the lid.
7. Puree the soup using an immersion blender until smooth and creamy. Serve and enjoy.

Nutrition:

Calories – 295 Protein – 7.7 g. Fat – 8.1 g. Carbs – 56.4 g.

Chickpea Air fryer Soup

Preparation Time: 10 minutes

Cooking Time: 25 minutes

Servings: 6

Ingredients:

- 2 cups of dry chickpeas
- 2 tablespoons extra virgin olive oil
- 3 garlic cloves, minced
- 1 yellow onion, chopped
- 2 carrots, chopped
- 1 green bell pepper, cored and chopped
- 3-4 red chili peppers
- 1 teaspoon ground coriander
- 1 teaspoon ground cumin
- a teaspoon of Aleppo pepper (A Middle Eastern spice)
- ½ teaspoon of ground turmeric
- ½ teaspoon of ground allspice

- 6 cups of low-sodium vegetable broth
- 15 ounces of chopped tomatoes with the juice
- juice from 1 lemon
- 1-ounce fresh cilantro, chopped
- salt to taste

Directions:

1. Place the dry chickpeas in a bowl and submerge them in water. Let them soak overnight and then drain well.
2. Preheat your air fryer using the saute setting and adjust the heat to high. Put in the extra virgin olive oil and heat until simmering. Add the onions, garlic, and a pinch of salt. Cook for 3 minutes, while stirring regularly.
3. Add the carrots, bell peppers, and spices. Cook for another 4 minutes, while stirring until the vegetables have softened a bit.
4. Add the chickpeas, tomatoes, and the broth. Make sure to add the juice from the tomatoes too. Lock the air fryer lid, and put the pressure cooking setting on high. Set a timer for 15 minutes.

5. After cooking, allow natural release of pressure. After 10 minutes, you can press the quick release to remove any extra pressure.
6. Carefully unlock and remove the lid. Mix in the lemon juice and fresh cilantro.
7. Transfer the contents to serving bowls and drizzle a little extra olive oil.

Nutrition:

Calories – 367 Protein – 20.1 g. Fat – 9.8 g. Carbs – 12.1 g.

Jalapeño Bacon Cheese Bread

Preparation Time: 25 minutes

Servings: 8 sticks

Ingredients:

- 2 large eggs.
- 4 slices sugar-free bacon; cooked and chopped
- ¼ cup chopped pickled jalapeños.
- ¼ cup grated Parmesan cheese.

- 2 cups shredded mozzarella cheese

Directions:

1. Mix all ingredients in a large bowl. Cut a piece of parchment to fit your air fryer basket.
2. Dampen your hands with a bit of water and press out the mixture into a circle. You may need to separate this into two smaller cheese breads, depending on the size of your fryer
3. Place the parchment and cheese bread into the air fryer basket
4. Adjust the temperature to 320 Degrees F and set the timer for 15 minutes. Carefully flip the bread when 5 minutes remain
5. When fully cooked, the top will be golden brown. Serve warm.

Nutrition:

Calories: 273; Protein: 20.1g; Fiber: 0.1g; Fat: 18.1g; Carbs: 2.3g

Ranch Dipped Fillets

Preparation Time: 5 minutes

Cooking Time: 13 minutes

Servings: 2

Ingredients:
- 1 egg beaten
- 2 tilapia fillets
- ¼ cup panko breadcrumbs
- Garnish: Herbs and chilies
- ½ packet ranch dressing mix powder
- 1¼ tablespoons vegetable oil

Directions:
1. Preheat the Air fryer to 350 degrees F and grease an Air fryer basket.
2. Mix ranch dressing with panko breadcrumbs in a bowl.
3. Whisk eggs in a shallow bowl and dip the fish fillet in the eggs.

4. Dredge in the breadcrumbs and transfer into the Air fryer basket.
5. Cook for about 13 minutes and garnish with chilies and herbs to serve.

Nutrition:

Calories: 301, Fat: 12.2g, Carbohydrates: 1.5g, Sugar: 1.4g, Protein: 28.8g, Sodium: 276mg

Zucchini Air Fried Gratin

Preparation Time: 10 minutes

Cooking Time: 15 minutes

Servings: 4

Ingredients:

- 2 zucchinis, cut into 8 equal sized pieces
- 2 tablespoons bread crumbs
- 1 tablespoon fresh parsley, chopped
- 4 tablespoons Parmesan cheese, grated
- 1 tablespoon vegetable oil
- Salt and black pepper, to taste

Directions:

1. Preheat the Air fryer to 360 degrees F and grease an Air fryer basket.
2. Arrange the zucchini pieces in the Air fryer basket with their skin side down.
3. Top with the remaining ingredients and cook for about 15 minutes.
4. Dish out and serve warm.

Nutrition:

Calories: 481, Fat: 11.1g, Carbohydrates: 9.1g, Sugar: 3g, Protein: 7g, Sodium: 203mg

Sweet Cream Cheese Wontons

Preparation Time: 5 minutes

Cooking Time: 5 minutes

Servings: 16

Ingredients:

- Wonton wrappers
- 1 egg with a little water

- ½ C. powdered erythritol
- 8 ounces softened cream cheese
- Olive oil

Directions:

1. Mix sweetener and cream cheese together.
2. Lay out 4 wontons at a time and cover with a dish towel to prevent drying out.
3. Place ½ of a teaspoon of cream cheese mixture into each wrapper.
4. Dip finger into egg/water mixture and fold diagonally to form a triangle. Seal edges well.
5. Repeat with remaining ingredients.
6. Place filled wontons into the air fryer oven and cook 5 minutes at 400 degrees, shaking halfway through cooking.

Nutrition:

Calories – 303, Protein – 0.5 g., Fat – 3 g., Carbs – 3 g.

Mini Lava Cakes

Preparation Time: 30 minutes

Servings: 4

Ingredients:
- 2 eggs, whisked
- 3 oz. dark chocolate; melted
- ¼ cup coconut oil; melted
- 1 tbsp. almond flour

- ¼ tsp. vanilla extract
- 2 tbsp. swerve
- Cooking spray

Directions:

1. In bowl, combine all the ingredients except the cooking spray and whisk really well.
2. Divide this into 4 ramekins greased with cooking spray, put them in the fryer and cook at 360°F for 20 minutes

Nutrition:

Calories: 161; Fat: 12g; Fiber: 1g; Carbs: 4g; Protein: 7g

Coconut Bars

Preparation Time: 5 minutes

Cooking time: 40 minutes

Servings: 12

Ingredients:
- 1 and ¼ cups almond flour
- 1 cup butter, melted
- 1 cup swerve
- ½ cup coconut cream
- 1 egg yolk
- 1 and ½ cups coconut, flaked
- ¾ cup walnuts, chopped
- ½ teaspoon vanilla extract

Directions:
1. In a bowl, mix the flour with half of the swerve and half of the butter, stir well and press this on the bottom of a baking pan that fits the air fryer.

2. Introduce this in the air fryer and cook at 350 degrees F for 15 minutes.
3. Meanwhile, heat up a pan with the rest of the butter over medium heat, add the remaining swerve and the rest of the Ingredients:, whisk, cook for 1-2 minutes, take off the heat and cool down.
4. Spread this well over the crust, put the pan in the air fryer again and cook at 350 degrees F for 25 minutes.
5. Cool down, cut into bars and serve.

Nutrition:

Calories 182, fat 12, fiber 2, carbs 4, protein 4

Cream Doughnuts

Preparation Time: 15 minutes

Cooking Time: 16 minutes

Servings: 8

Ingredients:

- 2 egg yolks
- 2¼ cups plain flour
- 4 tablespoons butter, softened and divided
- 1½ teaspoons baking powder
- ½ cup sugar
- 1 teaspoon salt
- ½ cup sour cream
- ½ cup heavy cream

Directions:

1. Preheat the Air fryer to 355 °F and grease an Air fryer basket lightly.
2. Sift together flour, baking powder and salt in a large bowl.

3. Add sugar and cold butter and mix until a coarse crumb is formed.
4. Stir in the egg yolks, ½ of the sour cream and 1/3 of the flour mixture and mix until a dough is formed.
5. Add remaining sour cream and 1/3 of the flour mixture and mix until well combined.
6. Stir in the remaining flour mixture and combine well.
7. Roll the dough into ½ inch thickness onto a floured surface and cut into donuts with a donut cutter.
8. Coat butter on both sides of the donuts and arrange in the Air fryer basket.
9. Cook for about 8 minutes until golden and top with heavy cream to serve.

Nutrition:

Calories: 297, Fats: 13g, Carbohydrates: 40.7g, Sugar: 12.6g, Proteins: 5g, Sodium: 346mg

Avocado Walnut Bread

Preparation Time: 5 minutes

Cooking Time: 35 minutes

Servings: 6

Ingredients:

- 2 large eggs, beaten
- ¾ cup: 3 oz. almond flour, white
- 2 ripe avocados, cored, peeled and mashed
- 2 tablespoons: 3/4 oz. Toasted walnuts, chopped roughly
- ¼ teaspoon baking soda
- 1 teaspoon cinnamon ground
- ½ teaspoon kosher salt
- 2 tablespoons vegetable oil
- ½ cup granulated swerve
- 1 teaspoon vanilla extract

Directions:

1. Preheat the Air fryer to 310 degrees F and line a 6-inch baking pan with parchment paper.
2. Mix almond flour, salt, baking soda and cinnamon in a bowl.
3. Whisk eggs with avocado mash, yogurt, swerve, oil, and vanilla in a bowl.
4. Stir in the almond flour mixture and mix until well combined.
5. Pour the batter evenly into the pan and top with the walnuts.
6. Place the baking pan into the Air fryer basket and cook for about 35 minutes.
7. Dish out in a platter and cut into slices to serve.

Nutrition:

Calories: 248, Fat: 15.7g, Carbohydrates: 8.4g, Sugar: 1.1g, Protein: 14.1g, Sodium: 94mg

Pumpkin Bars

Preparation Time: 10 minutes

Cooking Time: 25 minutes

Servings: 6

Ingredients:

- ¼ cup almond butter
- ½ cup coconut flour
- 1 tablespoon unsweetened almond milk
- ¾ teaspoon baking soda
- ½ cup dark sugar free chocolate chips, divided
- ¼ cup swerve
- 1 cup canned sugar free pumpkin puree
- 1 teaspoon cinnamon
- 1 teaspoon vanilla extract
- ¼ teaspoon nutmeg
- ½ teaspoon ginger
- 1/8 teaspoon salt
- 1/8 teaspoon ground cloves

Directions:

1. Preheat the Air fryer to 360 degrees F and layer a baking pan with wax paper.
2. Mix pumpkin puree, swerve, vanilla extract, milk, and butter in a bowl.
3. Combine coconut flour, spices, salt, and baking soda in another bowl.
4. Combine the two mixtures and mix well until smooth.
5. Add about 1/3 cup of the sugar-free chocolate chips and transfer this mixture into the baking pan.
6. Transfer into the Air fryer basket and cook for about 25 minutes.
7. Microwave the sugar-free chocolate bits on low heat and dish out the baked cake from the pan.
8. Top with melted chocolate and slice to serve.

Nutrition:

Calories: 249, Fat: 11.9g, Carbohydrates: 1.8g, Sugar: 0.3g, Protein: 5g, Sodium: 79mg

Cinnamon Doughnuts

Preparation Time: 10 minutes

Cooking Time: 12 minutes

Servings: 6

Ingredients:

- 1 cup white almond flour
- 1 teaspoon baking powder
- 2 tablespoons water
- ¼ cup almond milk
- ¼ cup swerve
- 1 tablespoon coconut oil, melted
- 2 teaspoons cinnamon
- ½ teaspoon salt

Directions:

1. Preheat the Air fryer to 360 degrees F and grease an Air fryer basket.
2. Mix flour, swerve, salt, cinnamon and baking powder in a bowl.

3. Stir in the coconut oil, water, and soy milk until a smooth dough is formed.
4. Cover this dough and refrigerate for about 1 hour.
5. Mix ground cinnamon with 2 tablespoons swerve in another bowl and keep aside.
6. Divide the dough into 12 equal balls and roll each ball in the cinnamon swerve mixture.
7. Transfer 6 balls in the Air fryer basket and cook for about 6 minutes.
8. Repeat with the remaining balls and dish out to serve.

Nutrition:

Calories: 166, Fat: 4.9g, Carbohydrates: 9.3g, Sugar: 2.7g, Protein: 2.4g, Sodium: 3mg

Strawberry Tart

Preparation Time: 5 minutes

Cooking time: 20 minutes

Servings: 8

Ingredients:

- 2 cups strawberries, sliced
- 5 egg whites
- 1/3 cup swerve
- 1 and ½ cups almond flour

- Zest of 1 lemon, grated
- 1 teaspoon baking powder
- 1 teaspoon vanilla extract
- 1/3 cup butter, melted
- Cooking spray

Directions:

1. In a bowl, whisk egg whites well.
2. Add the rest of the Ingredients: except the cooking spray gradually and whisk everything.
3. Grease a tart pan with the cooking spray, and pour the strawberries mix.
4. Put the pan in the air fryer and cook at 370 degrees F for 20 minutes.
5. Cool down, slice and serve.

Nutrition:

Calories 182, fat 12, fiber 1, carbs 6, protein 5

Rum Cheesecake

Preparation Time: 30 minutes

Servings: 6

Ingredients:

- 2 eggs
- 16 oz. cream cheese; softened
- 1/2 tsp. vanilla extract
- 1/2 cup sugar

- 1/2 cup graham cookies; crumbled
- 2 tsp. butter; melted
- 1 tsp. rum

Directions:

1. Grease a pan with the butter and spread the cookie crumbs on the bottom.
2. In a bowl, mix all the remaining ingredients and whisk well; then spread this mixture over the cookie crumbs
3. Place the pan in your air fryer and cook at 340 °F for 20 minutes. Let the cheesecake cool down, refrigerate and serve cold

Apple Pie

Servings: 6

Preparation Time: 15 minutes

Cooking Time: 30 minutes

Ingredients

- 1 frozen pie crust, thawed
- 1 large apple, peeled, cored and chopped
- 3 tablespoons sugar, divided

- 2 teaspoons fresh lemon juice
- 1 tablespoon ground cinnamon
- ½ teaspoon vanilla extract
- 1 tablespoon butter, chopped
- 1 egg, beaten

Directions:
1. Grease a pie pan.
2. With a smaller baking tin, cut 1 crust from thawed pie crust about 1/8-inch larger than pie pan.
3. Now, cut the second crust from the pie crust a little smaller than first one.
4. Arrange the large crust in the bottom of the prepared pie pan.
5. In a bowl, mix together the apple, 2 tablespoons of sugar, cinnamon, lemon juice, and vanilla extract.
6. Place apple mixture evenly over the bottom crust.
7. Add the chopped butter over apple mixture.

8. Arrange the second crust on top and pinch the edges to seal.
9. Carefully, cut 3-4 slits in the top crust.
10. Spread the beaten egg evenly over top crust and sprinkle with the remaining sugar.
11. Set the temperature of air fryer to 320 degrees F.
12. Arrange the pie pan into an air fryer basket.
13. Air fry for about 30 minutes.
14. Remove from air fryer and place the pie pan onto a wire rack to cool for about 10-15 minutes before serving.
15. Serve warm.

Nutrition:

Calories: 190, Carbohydrate: 25.3g, Protein: 11.3g, Fat: 3.1g, Sugar: 1.6g, Sodium: 160mg

Coco Mug Cake

Preparation Time: 30 minutes

Servings: 1

Ingredients:

- 1 large egg.
- 2 tbsp. coconut flour.
- 2 tbsp. granular erythritol.
- 2 tbsp. heavy whipping cream.
- ¼ tsp. baking powder.
- ¼ tsp. vanilla extract.

Directions:

1. In a 4-inch ramekin, whisk egg, then add remaining ingredients. Stir until smooth. Place into the air fryer basket.
2. Adjust the temperature to 300 Degrees F and set the timer for 25 minutes.
3. When done a toothpick should come out clean. Enjoy right out of the ramekin with a spoon. Serve warm.

Nutrition:

Calories: 237; Protein: 9.9g; Fiber: 5.0g; Fat: 16.4g; Carbs: 40.7g

Notes

www.ingramcontent.com/pod-product-compliance
Lightning Source LLC
Chambersburg PA
CBHW070933080526
44589CB00013B/1503